IF FOUND PLE

C000077370

👤 _____

✉ _____

📱 _____

GREATER THAN A TOURIST BOOK SERIES
REVIEWS FROM READERS

I think the series is wonderful and beneficial for tourists to get information before visiting the city.

-Seckin Zumbul, Izmir Turkey

I am a world traveler who has read many trip guides but this one really made a difference for me. I would call it a heartfelt creation of a local guide expert instead of just a guide.

-Susy, Isla Holbox, Mexico

New to the area like me, this is a must have!

-Joe, Bloomington, USA

This is a good series that gets down to it when looking for things to do at your destination without having to read a novel for just a few ideas.

-Rachel, Monterey, USA

Good information to have to plan my trip to this destination.

-Pennie Farrell, Mexico

Great ideas for a port day.

-Mary Martin USA

Aptly titled, you won't just be a tourist after reading this book. You'll be greater than a tourist!

-Alan Warner, Grand Rapids, USA

Even though I only have three days to spend in San Miguel in an upcoming visit, I will use the author's suggestions to guide some of my time there. An easy read - with chapters named to guide me in directions I want to go.

-Robert Catapano, USA

Great insights from a local perspective! Useful information and a very good value!

-Sarah, USA

This series provides an in-depth experience through the eyes of a local. Reading these series will help you to travel the city in with confidence and it'll make your journey a unique one.

-Andrew Teoh, Ipoh, Malaysia

GREATER THAN A TOURIST – VANCOUVER BRITISH COLUMBIA CANADA

50 Travel Tips from a Local

CRISTINA LUTCAN

Cover designed by: Ivana Stamenkovic
Cover Image: https://pixabay.com/en/vancouver-british-columbia-canada-1620772/

Greater Than a Tourist
Visit our website at www.GreaterThanaTourist.com

Lock Haven, PA
ISBN: 9781983308666

>TOURIST

50 TRAVEL TIPS FROM A LOCAL

BOOK DESCRIPTION

Are you excited about planning your next trip?

Do you want to try something new?

Would you like some guidance from a local?

If you answered yes to any of these questions, then this Greater Than a Tourist book is for you.

Greater Than a Tourist- Vancouver British Columbia Canada by Cristina Lutcan offers the inside scoop on Vancouver. Most travel books tell you how to travel like a tourist. Although there is nothing wrong with that, as part of the Greater Than a Tourist series, this book will give you travel tips from someone who has lived at your next travel destination.

In these pages, you will discover advice that will help you throughout your stay. This book will not tell you exact addresses or store hours but instead will give you excitement and knowledge from a local that you may not find in other smaller print travel books.

Travel like a local. Slow down, stay in one place, and get to know the people and the culture. By the time you finish this book, you will be eager and prepared to travel to your next destination.

TABLE OF CONTENTS

12. BC Sports Hall of Fame
13. Outdoor Free Movies in Stanley Park
14. Festival of Lights
15. Vancouver Art Gallery
16. H.R. MacMillan Space Centre
17. Gastown & The Steam Clock
18. Davie Street
19. Yaletown
20. Beaver Lake in Stanley Park
21. RIO Theatre
22. 6pack Indoor Beach
23. Geocaching around the city
24. The Shameful Tiki Room
25. The Dark Table
26. Habitat Island
27. Rennie Collection Museum
28. Hot Art Wet City
29. Catfe
30. Macleod's Books
31. Everett Crowley Park
32. Kitsilano Beach
33. The Richmond Olympic Experience
34. Bloedel Conservatory
35. Beaty Biodiversity Museum
36. UBC Botanical Garden
37. Museum of Anthropology

DEDICATION

Dedicated to all the adventurers at heart who never stop seeking exciting experiences and are not afraid to overcome the fear of the unknown. Also, to my family.

ABOUT THE AUTHOR

Cristina is a blogger and world traveler who recently moved to Toronto from Vancouver, BC. She loves to read, laugh and dance when nobody's watching. Her footsteps left marks in 15 countries and she's not planning to stop anytime soon. Vancouver is the place where her true creative spirit came into existence, that's why it holds a special place in her heart.

HOW TO USE THIS BOOK

The Greater Than a Tourist book series was written by someone who has lived in an area for over three months. The goal of this book is to help travelers either dream or experience different locations by providing opinions from a local. The author has made suggestions based on their own experiences. Please do your own research before traveling to the area in case the suggested places are unavailable.

FROM THE PUBLISHER

Traveling can be one of the most important parts of a person's life. The anticipation and memories that you have are some of the best. As a publisher of the Greater Than a Tourist book series, as well as the popular 50 Things to Know book series, we strive to help you learn about new places, spark your imagination, and inspire you. Wherever you are and whatever you do I wish you safe, fun, and inspiring travel.

Lisa Rusczyk Ed. D.
CZYK Publishing

OUR STORY

Traveling is a passion of the "Greater than a Tourist" series creator. Lisa studied abroad in college, and for their honeymoon Lisa and her husband toured Europe. During her travels to Malta, an older man tried to give her some advice based on his own experience living on the island since he was a young boy. She was not sure if she should talk to the stranger but was interested in his advice. When traveling to some places she was wary to talk to locals because she was afraid that they weren't being genuine. Through her travels, Lisa learned how much locals had to share with tourists. Lisa created the "Greater Than a Tourist" book series to help connect people with locals. A topic that locals are very passionate about sharing.

WELCOME TO
> TOURIST

INTRODUCTION

"Not until we are lost do we begin to understand ourselves"
– Henry David Thoreau

It's called "The Best Place on Earth" for a reason. And if your heart is itching for adventures, you know you have found your perfect destination. Welcome to the home of hockey, world class mountains, and relaxing beaches. You're going to love it here.

1. WATERFRONT AND THE OLYMPIC CAULDRON

Popular landmark that you can't miss. Check out the massive Cruise Ships that dock in the harbor during summer time, stop by Fly Over Canada attraction for a fun, virtual flight above this beautiful land or visit the famous Olympic Cauldron and "The Drop" Sculpture resembling a raindrop that brings a homage to the power of nature. Don't forget to look up to the mountains where you'll see Seymour, Cypress and Grouse mountain peaks.

2. SUNSET BEACH

You will often hear about English Bay when it comes to popular beaches in Vancouver. I recommend you visit Sunset Beach which is only a few miles away from English Bay's crowds and gives you a perfect view of the Burrard Bridge and the Granville Island. Soak your feet in the water, take a picture in front of the massive "Engagement" sculpture made by renowned artist Dennis Oppenheim or lay down on the grass with a good book in your hands.

3. GRANVILLE ISLAND

If you like local arts and crafts and looking to acquire some personalized gifts for yourself or your loved ones, start with taking a cute and cheap AquaBus to Granville Island. Here, treat yourself to a fun Improv Show, sample some tasty beer at the local Brewery, or soak in the sun while enjoying the Vancouver downtown skyline from the other side of the shore.

4. BIKE THE SEAWALL

If you choose to visit Vancouver in summer-time, I suggest you rent a bike and get to know downtown and the Seawall on 2 wheels. Find a map of the area at any hotel or just bike down to the water, choose one direction and let the adventure begin. It's a fun way to spend a sunny day while seeing as much of Vancouver as possible.

5. HIKE THE BURNABY MOUNTAIN

Tough challenge that rewards you with a beautiful sight of downtown Vancouver the moment you reach the top. The hike can be completed in under 2 hours, however be prepared for an endless stairwell to heaven. At the top, you can relax in the on-site restaurant, check out the lumber-jack show or visit the resident bears- Grinder and Coola.

6. STALK YOUR FAVORITE MOVIE STAR OR MOVIE PROJECT

Ok, it's not really stalking but Vancouver is considered a prime location in the film industry and has thousands of productions filmed there every year. The list is always available online, so check out where you favorite actors are and pay a visit to the set. You might even be lucky to get a picture or a personalized autograph.

7. SCIENCE WORLD AT TELUS WORLD OF SCIENCE

This place is a treat no matter how old you are. Here you can find a whole world of curiosity including interactive displays, exhibitions and amazing science shows. The facility also has the world's largest domed OMNIMAX screen that projects fascinating movies daily.

8. CAPILANO SUSPENSION BRIDGE

Yes, it's packed with tourists especially during the high season, but I guarantee – you will love this place. Take the free shuttle from Waterfront – that includes a free guided tour of downtown and 30 min later you'll find yourself on the longest Suspension Bridge in North America. The park also includes the seven bridges of Treetops Adventure and the thrilling Cliffwalk. Reserve 2-3h to explore this beautiful place.

9. ROBSON SQUARE

Dance in Summer or Skate in Winter. One of my favorite places in downtown, Robson Square is always bustling with creativity and life. There are free dance classes throughout summer – you don't have to be a pro or have a partner- the dance teachers will show you all the moves. In winter, the free skate rink is open daily with life shows and good music. Bring your own skates or rent a pair for only $4, get out there and show-case your skating skills.

10. VANCOUVER AQUARIUM

The Aquarium brings me back to Finding Dory's Marine Life Institute, with all the dedicated staff that works daily to take care of all the permanent residents. Here you'll find penguins, adorable sea otters and 50,000 other aquatic creatures that call this place home. Daily shows will keep you entertained and the 4D Experience Theatre, will offer you a full immersion in the Marine World.

11. PROSPECT POINT STANLEY PARK

A well-kept secret that is still not widely known amongst tourists. I recommend you visit this place just before sunset, so you can catch the changing lights in the sky but also to notice how the city enters the night mode. The viewpoint is located in Stanley Park – you can bike, walk or drive there. It's an iconic location that overlooks Lions Gate Bridge, Burrard Inlet and the North Shore Mountains.

12. BC SPORTS HALL OF FAME

You don't have to be a sports fan to visit this massive place. Learn about Canada's sports history while celebrating best athletes and teams in a fun and interactive way. Here you'll find out more about the 2010 Olympics, Canucks, BC Lions or Vancouver's Whitecaps teams that has Canadians cheering up for at every game.

13. OUTDOOR FREE MOVIES IN STANLEY PARK

Travelers know about Stanley Park as being the popular outdoors destination in downtown Vancouver. Over the summer, however, Second Beach brings together thousands of people in front of a massive outdoor screen to watch classics or movies loved by entire generations. Bring a blanket, some snacks and make sure you arrive a little earlier for prime seating. Oh, and watch out for the friendly skunks – they seem to have a big love for movies too.

14. FESTIVAL OF LIGHTS

If you visit Vancouver in the month of August – absolutely don't miss this event as it's one of the most spectacular display of fireworks in the world. Every year, 3 countries compete in this fireworks competition that happens over the course of a week for 30min assigned to every country. The event attracts a crowd of half a million people, so make sure you arrive early to secure a good seat (in front of Cactus Club) as the music for the show is provided in front of that location.

15. VANCOUVER ART GALLERY

Centrally located right in the heart of downtown, here you can immerse yourself in famous and historic works of art and countless contemporary exhibitions that are sure to leave a lasting effect on you. The gallery holds over 10,000 pieces of art in its permanent collection and has countless traveling exhibits on display. You have the option of a guided gallery tour or just explore the exhibits at your own pace.

16. H.R. MACMILLAN SPACE CENTRE

If you have a fascination with the sky, make sure you visit the Space Centre to get an insight in the infinite of the universe. Check out the centre's movies for a full immersive experience in the depths of our universe.

17. GASTOWN & THE STEAM CLOCK

Trendy neighborhood, having been the original townsite from which Vancouver grew in the 1870's. Here you'll find countless coffee shops, Victorian era streets and the world famous Steam Clock that whistles and shoots steam every quarter hour.

18. DAVIE STREET

We all know how proud Canada of its multi-culturalism and its inclusion of all LGBTQ+ people. The heart of Davie str. has a beautiful rainbow crosswalk and you'll often notice the rainbow flags displayed on windows from homes or businesses alike. If you're here in summer time, don't miss the popular Pride Parade.

19. YALETOWN

The fancy, up-scale neighborhood. Here you'll find upscale restaurants and shops just steps away from the seawall. The perfect spot to take the Aqua Bus to Granville Island or to start your bicycle tour.

20. BEAVER LAKE IN STANLEY PARK

Leave the safety of the seawall and adventure inside Stanley Park on one of their hiking trails that will take you to this serene lake. Walk, roller blade or bike to get here, and then enjoy a lovely afternoon surrounded by nature.

21. RIO THEATRE

Forget the regular theatres, RIO will offer you a complete immersive experience in the movie world if you get lucky to see one of the popular Cult movies. Interact with the screen, throw paper on the stage and externalize your frustration with an annoying character. You are allowed.

22. 6PACK INDOOR BEACH

It's exactly how it sounds like. Huge warehouse full of sand, volleyball nets, archery tag and good drinks. Perfect way to spend a rainy day (and Vancouver gets a lot of rainy days).

23. GEOCACHING AROUND THE CITY

It's quite universal but it's even more fun when it comes to a big city like Vancouver. There are countless of mystery boxed hidden in the area by adventurers alike. It's never a bad time for a treasure hunt.

24. THE SHAMEFUL TIKI ROOM

Popular venue that offers exotic drinks and food with an eclectic atmosphere. Find this hidden place for a getaway from the regular city entertainment options. Get transported into another world while listening to enchanting live music.

25. THE DARK TABLE

That's right, dinner in the dark while served by blind waiters is the new trend in Vancouver and it's amazing. I recommend you choose the 3-course chef's surprise menu for a full immersive experience. Make sure your friends are talkative as in the absence of light, everyone will compensate with plenty of talking.

26. HABITAT ISLAND

Urban sanctuary along the popular False Creek. Here you'll find insects, crabs, starfish, barnacles and a variety of birds especially during high tide. Walk amongst trees and flowers and enjoy a beautiful afternoon relaxing near the water.

27. RENNIE COLLECTION MUSEUM

By-appointment gallery that provides a knowledgeable tour of one of Canada's largest contemporary art collections. The tours last 90 min and you can register on the official website. Located inside the oldest building in Chinatown so make sure you don't mis this unique spot.

28. HOT ART WET CITY

Fun, quirky art gallery that hosts comedy shows, drawing classes and workshops that are not exactly very mainstream. You'll find intricate arts of work, artists without inhibitions and loud collections of narrative work.

29. CATFE

If you're a fan of the furry animals, then the Cat Café is the perfect spot for a coffee and a good snuggle with your favorite felines. The cats are all up for adoption (if you need a furry friend), however if you're looking to just enjoy their company, feel free to make a reservation and visit the purrfect creatures. Walk-ins are limited in a day, so I recommend to making a reservation in advance.

30. MACLEOD'S BOOKS

For the bookworm lover, this place is stacked with hundreds of books from modern to antique. Swap your books, get to know the owner or ask the staff to dig out your next golden book. Be warned: if you're an avid reader, you might be stuck here until sunset.

31. EVERETT CROWLEY PARK

Hidden on the Vancouver's East side, this park saw light from a former garbage dump spot in the 60's. Since then, the land went through a major makeover becoming a true nature sanctuary. If you love puppies, here is the place where you'll see a lot of them.

32. KITSILANO BEACH

One of the most popular beaches in the area, you will find it packed with people especially in summertime. It offers panoramic views of downtown Vancouver, Burrard Inlet and the North Shore Mountains. You'll find restaurants and parks in the area so make sure you book at least half-day for exploration.

33. THE RICHMOND OLYMPIC EXPERIENCE

Most of us will never get to compete in the Olympics. You can get the experience at the Olympic Oval which is just a short skytrain ride from downtown. Feel the rush as you fly off an Olympic Ski Jump, paddle down an adventurous white-water rafting course or check out the bobsleigh track. Either way, it's bound to be an unforgettable experience.

34. BLOEDEL CONSERVATORY

Right at the top of the Queen Elizabeth Park where you get a view of downtown Vancouver. Indoor location perfect for those rainy days. Discover 120 exotic birds and over 500 types of tropical plants inside the giant dome.

35. BEATY BIODIVERSITY MUSEUM

Located on the UBC Campus, this museum explores Vancouver's natural history. It displays birds, insects, fish, plants and a giant suspended whale skeleton. Make sure you watch the educational movies to find out more about the flora and fauna of this area.

36. UBC BOTANICAL GARDEN

While you're visiting the massive UBC Campus, stop by this botanical garden. Here you'll find the Nitobe Memorial Garden and the Greenheart TreeWalk. Vancouverites have an innate love for Treewalks. It's truly a lot of fun.

37. MUSEUM OF ANTHROPOLOGY

Another great spot for your creative heart. Explore contemporary and traditional art from Canada's First Nations and other cultures around the world. All while overlooking the mountains and the sea.

38. DR. SUN YAT-SEN CLASSICAL CHINESE GARDEN

You can't skip Chinatown when you're in Vancouver. This Ming-Dynasty garden-home feels like a true paradise. Enjoy the complimentary walking tour, get a refreshing drink, admire the art displayed and discover a beautiful forgotten world.

39. BURNABY VILLAGE MUSEUM AND CAROUSEL

Go back in time when the year is 1920. Explore the tram and the old village. Don't forget to bring your child within to life by riding the vintage carousel and enjoying a sweet treat from the Ice Cream Parlor.

40. BILL REID GALLERY OF NORTHWEST COAST ART

Located in the heart of downtown, the gallery is home to special exhibitions of contemporary Indigenous Art of the Northwest Coast being the only museum of its kind on the west coast. Learn about Indigenous cultures, values and the diverse style of life that shaped a major part of Canadian history.

41. THE MARINE BUILDING

Considered one of the world's most exquisite examples of art deco architecture, the building opened in 1930 and it was considered the tallest building in the British Empire. You might recognize it from the

Fantastic Four films, Smallville or as the Clark Kent's workplace.

42. VANCOUVER POLICE MUSEUM

Looking to find yourself in a "safe" dangerous situation? This museum explores the history of crime, law enforcement and death investigation, all located in the old Coroner's Court & City Morgue. You can opt for "Sins of the City" themed tour offered by the museum and dive deeper in the underworld creepy stories of Vancouver.

43. THE WRECK BEACH

Full disclaimer: It's a nude beach. You don't have to leave your clothes at home but don't be surprised if people walk around in their natural attires. There are also events organized during the year, so you don't feel out of place if you do decide to be a little more adventurous. Relax, have fun and make sure to make new friends along the way.

44. DUDE CHILLING PARK

Wouldn't this make a fun picture for your social media accounts? The park got the nickname from a piece of art by sculptor Michael Dennis titled: Reclining Figure that was a fun vision of just some dude relaxing. 1500 petitions had to be signed for the park to be renamed and until this days remains a reason to smile for all the passers-by.

45. THE SAM KEE (JACK CHOW) BUILDING

Considered the world's narrowest freestanding office building, being inducted in the Guinness World Records, as it's only six feet two inches deep. Rumor has it that there is a secret tunnel that runs underneath the basement that connects with a near-by alley. Who doesn't like a narrow, old building surrounded by mystery?

46. MUSEUM OF VANCOUVER

A visual feast of innovation and tradition, what's more unique about this museum is here you'll find a collection of Neon signs dating from the 1950 through to 1970's. If you're a fan of the good old days of huge, colorful signs and that vintage atmosphere, this is a place you should not miss.

47. 9 O'CLOCK GUN

While exploring Stanley Park, make sure you arrive at this historic landmark close to 9pm. In the past it was used to alert salmon fishermen that the workday was coming to an end. This piece of naval artillery erupts every evening sending shockwaves blasting across the inner harbor to passers-by delight.

48. YALETOWN BREWING COMPANY

Vancouverites love their beer, so you'll often find this tavern-style bar, full of people. The brewery features rotating taps of house brews and organizes weekly batch testing of new brews. Grab two pieces of ID and enjoy a fun night out with your friends.

49. LIGHTHOUSE PARK

Retreat from the bustling life of downtown in this gorgeous park in West Vancouver. You'll find yourself surrounded by 500 years old trees that stand

200 feet tall. Explore the hiking trails and visit the old Point Atkinson lighthouse, a National Historic Site of Canada.

50. CAMBIE CLIMBING TREE

You are right, I saved the best for the last. This secret spot, perfect for climbing has branches that are perfectly spaced out for access to its upper reaches (and I know you're brave enough). You'll find a hammock or a swing on the top to enjoy the sights and to look at the world below you. Located near the Cambie Bridge, overlooking the North Shore Mountains.

TOP REASONS TO BOOK THIS TRIP

Multi-culturalism: Meet and make friends from all around the world.

Outdoor Activities: Mountains, lakes and the ocean – what else can you ask for?

Diverse neighborhoods: You can't be bored here.

BONUS BOOK

50 THINGS TO KNOW ABOUT PACKING LIGHT FOR TRAVEL

PACK THE RIGHT WAY EVERY TIME

AUTHOR: MANIDIPA BHATTACHARYYA

Edited by Melanie Howthorne

ABOUT THE AUTHOR

Manidipa Bhattacharyya is a creative writer and editor, with an education in English literature and Linguistics. After working in the IT industry for seven long years she decided to call it quits and follow her heart instead. Manidipa has been ghost writing, editing, proof reading and doing secondary research services for many story tellers and article writers for about three years. She stays in Kolkata, India with her husband and a busy two year old. In her own time Manidipa enjoys travelling, photography and writing flash fiction.

Manidipa believes in travelling light and never carries anything that she couldn't haul herself on a trip. However, travelling with her child changed the scenario. She seemed to carry the entire world with her for the baby on the first two trips. But good sense prevailed and she is again working her way to becoming a light traveler, this time with a kid.

INTRODUCTION

He who would travel happily
must travel light.

-Antoine de Saint-Exupéry

Travel takes you to different places from seas and mountains to deserts and much more. In your travels you get to interact with different people and their cultures. You will, however, enjoy the sights and interact positively with these new people even more, if you are travelling light.

When you travel light your mind can be free from worry about your belongings. You do not have to spend precious vacation time waiting for your luggage to arrive after a long flight. There is be no chance of your bags going missing and the best part is that you need not pay a fee for checked baggage.

People who have mastered this art of packing light will root for you to take only one carry-on, wherever you go. However, many people can find it really hard to pack light. More so if you are travelling with children. Differentiating between "must have" and "just in case" items is the starting point. There will be ample shopping avenues at your destination which are just waiting to be explored.

This book will show you 'packing' in a new 'light' –
pun intended – and help you to embrace light
packing practices for all of your future travels.

Off to packing!

DEDICATION

I dedicate this book to all the travel buffs that I know,
who have given me great insights into the contents of
their backpacks.

THE RIGHT TRAVEL GEAR

1. CHOOSE YOUR TRAVEL GEAR CAREFULLY

While selecting your travel gear, pick items that are
light weight, durable and most importantly, easy to
carry. There are cases with wheels so you can drag
them along – these are usually on the heavy side
because of the trolley. Alternatively a backpack that
you can carry comfortably on your back, or even a
duffel bag that you can carry easily by hand or sling
across your body are also great options. Whatever
you choose, one thing to keep in mind is that the
luggage itself should not weigh a ton, this will give
you the flexibility to bring along one extra pair of
shoes if you so desire.

2. CARRY THE MINIMUM NUMBER OF BAGS

Selecting light weight luggage is not everything. You need to restrict the number of bags you carry as well. One carry-on size bag is ideal for light travel. Most carriers allow one cabin baggage plus one purse, handbag or camera bag as long as it slides under the seat in front. So technically, you can carry two items of luggage without checking them in.

3. PACK ONE EXTRA BAG

Always pack one extra empty bag along with your essential items. This could be a very light weight duffel bag or even a sturdy tote bag which takes up minimal space. In the event that you end up buying a lot of souvenirs, you already have a handy bag to stuff all that into and do not have to spend time hunting for an appropriate bag.

I'm very strict with my packing and have everything in its right place. I never change a rule. I hardly use anything in the hotel room. I wheel my own wardrobe in and that's it.

Charlie Watts

CLOTHES & ACCESSORIES

4. PLAN AHEAD

Figure out in advance what you plan to do on your trip. That will help you to pick that one dress you need for the occasion. If you are going to attend a wedding then you have to carry formal wear. If not, you can ditch the gown for something lighter that will be comfortable during long walks or on the beach.

5. WEAR THAT JACKET

Remember that wearing items will not add extra luggage for your air travel. So wear that bulky jacket that you plan to carry for your trip. This saves space and can also help keep you warm during the chilly flight.

6. MIX AND MATCH

Carry clothes that can be interchangeably used to reinvent your look. Find one top that goes well with a couple of pairs of pants or skirts. Use tops, shirts and jackets wisely along with other accessories like a scarf or a stole to create a new look.

7. CHOOSE YOUR FABRIC WISELY

Stuffing clothes in cramped bags definitely takes its toll which results in wrinkles. It is best to carry wrinkle free, synthetic clothes or merino tops. This will eliminate the need for that small iron you usually bring along.

8. DITCH CLOTHES PACK UNDERWEAR

Pack more underwear and socks. These are the things that will give you a fresh feel even if you do not get a chance to wear fresh clothes. Moreover these are easy to wash and can be dried inside the hotel room itself.

9. CHOOSE DARK OVER LIGHT

While picking your clothes choose dark coloured ones. They are easy to colour coordinate and can last longer before needing a wash. Accidental food spills and dirt from the road are less visible on darker clothes.

10. WEAR YOUR JEANS

Take only one pair of Jeans with you, which you should wear on the flight. Remember to pick a pair that can be worn for sightseeing trips and is equally eloquent for dinner. You can add variety by adding light weight cargoes and chinos.

11. CARRY SMART ACCESSORIES

The right accessory can give you a fresh look even with the same old dress. An intelligent neck-piece, a couple of bright scarves, stoles or a sarong can be used in a number of ways to add variety to your clothing. These light weight beauties can double up as a nursing cover, a light blanket, beach wear, a modesty cover for visiting places of worship, and also makes for an enthralling game of peek-a-boo.

12. LEARN TO FOLD YOUR GARMENTS

Seasoned travellers all swear by rolling their clothes for compact and wrinkle free packing. Bundle packing, where you roll the clothes around a central object as if tying it up, is also a popular method of compact and wrinkle free packing. Stacking folded clothes one on top of another is a big no-no as it makes creases extreme and they are difficult to get rid of without ironing.

13. WASH YOUR DIRTY LAUNDRY

One of the ways to avoid carrying loads of clothes is to wash the clothes you carry. At some places you might get to use the laundry services or a Laundromat but if you are in a pinch, best solution is to wash them yourself. If that is the plan then carrying quick drying clothes is highly recommended, which most often also happen to be the wrinkle free variety.

14. LEAVE THOSE TOWELS BEHIND

Regular towels take up a lot of space, are heavy and take ages to dry out. If you are staying at hotels they will provide you with towels anyway. If you are travelling to a remote place, where the availability of towels look doubtful, carry a light weight travel towel of viscose material to do the job.

15. USE A COMPRESSION BAG

Compression bags are getting lots of recommendation now days from regular travellers. These are useful for saving space in your luggage when you have to pack bulky dresses. While packing for the return trip, get help from the hotel staff to arrange a vacuum cleaner.

FOOTWEAR

16. PUT ON YOUR HIKING BOOTS

If you have plans to go hiking or trekking during your trip, you will need those bulky hiking boots. The best way to carry them is to wear them on flight to save space and luggage weight. You can remove the boots once inside and be comfortable in your socks.

17. PICKING THE RIGHT SHOES

Shoes are often the bulkiest items, along with being the dainty if you are a female. They need care and take up a lot of space in your luggage. It is advisable therefore to pick shoes very carefully. If you plan to do a lot of walking and site seeing, then wearing a pair of comfortable walking shoes are a must. For more formal occasions you can carry durable, light weight flats which will not take up much space.

18. STUFF SHOES

If you happen to pack a pair of shoes, ensure you utilize their hollow insides. Tuck small items like rolled up socks or belts to save space. They will also be easy to find.

TOILETRIES

19. STASHING TOILETRIES

Carry only absolute necessities. Airline rules dictate that for one carry-on bag, liquids and gels must be in 3.4 ounce (100ml) bottles or less, and must be packed in a one quart zip-lock bag. If you are planning to stay in a hotel, the basic things will be provided for you. It's best is to buy the rest from the local market at your destination.

20. TAKE ALONG TAMPONS

Tampons are a hard to find item in a lot of countries. Figure out how many you need and pack accordingly. For longer stays you can buy them online and have them delivered to where you are staying.

21. GET PAMPERED BEFORE YOU TRAVEL

Some avid travellers suggest getting a pedicure and manicure just the day before travelling. This not only gives you a well kept look, you also save the trouble of packing nail polish. Remember, every little bit of weight reduced adds up.

ELECTRONICS
22. LUGGING ALONG ELECTRONICS

Electronics have a large role to play in our lives today. Most of us cannot imagine our lives away from our phones, laptops or tablets. However while travelling, one must consider the amount of weight these electronics add to our luggage. Thankfully smart phones come along with all the essentials tools like a camera, email access, picture editing tools and more. They are smart to the point of eliminating the need to carry multiple gadgets. Choose a smart phone that suits all your requirements and travel with the world in your palms or pocket.

23. REDUCE THE NUMBER OF CHARGERS

If you do travel with multiple electronic devices, you will have to bear the additional burden of carrying all their chargers too. Check if a single charger can be used for multiple devices. You might also consider investing in a pocket charger. These small devices support multiple devices while keeping you charged on the go.

24. TRAVEL FRIENDLY APPS

Along with smart phones come numerous apps, which are immensely helpful in our travels. You name it and you have an app for it at hand – take pictures, sharing with friends and family, torch to light dark roads, maps, checking flight/train times, find hotels and many other things. Use these smart alternatives to traditional items like books to eliminate weight and save space.

I get ideas about what's essential when packing my suitcase.

-Diane von Furstenberg

TRAVELLING WITH KIDS

25. BRING ALONG THE STROLLER

Kids might enjoy walking for a while but they soon tire out and a stroller is the just the right thing for them to rest in while you continue your tour. Strollers also double duty as a luggage carrier and shopping bag holder. Remember to pick a light weight, easy to handle brand of stroller. Better yet, find out in advance if you can rent a stroller at your destination.

26. BRING ONLY ENOUGH DIAPERS FOR YOUR TRIP

Diapers take up a lot of space and add to the weight of your luggage. Therefore it is advisable to carry just enough diapers to last through the trip and a few for afterwards, till you buy fresh stock at your destination. Unless of course you are travelling to a really remote area, in which case you have no choice but to carry the load. Otherwise diapers are something you will find pretty easily.

27. TAKE ONLY A COUPLE OF TOYS

Children are easily attracted by new things in their environment. While travelling they will find numerous 'new' objects to scrutinize and play with. Packing just one favorite toy is enough, or if there is no favorite toy leave out all of them in favor of stories or imaginary games.

28. CARRY KID FRIENDLY SNACKS

Create a small snack counter in your bag to store away quick bites for those sudden hunger pangs. Depending on the child's age this could include chocolates, raisins, dry fruits, granola bars or biscuits. Also keep a bottle of water handy for your little one.

These things do not add much weight and can be adjusted in a handbag or knapsack.

29. GAMES TO CARRY

Create some travel specific, imaginary games if you have slightly grown up children, like spot the attractions. Keep a coloring book and colors handy for in-flight or hotel time. Apps on your smart phone can keep the children engaged with cartoons and story books. Older children are often entertained by games available on phones or tablets. This cuts the weight of luggage down while keeping the kids entertained.

30. LET THE KIDS CARRY THEIR LOAD

A good thing is to start early sharing of responsibilities. Let your child pick a bag of his or her choice and pack it themselves. Keep tabs on what they are stuffing in their bags by asking if they will be using that item on the trip. It could start out being just an entertainment bag initially but with growing years they will learn to sort the useful from the superfluous. Children as little as four can maneuver a small trolley suitcase like a pro- their experience in pull along toys credit. If you are worried that you may be pulling it for them, you may want to start with a backpack.

31. DECIDE ON LOCATION FOR CHILDREN TO SLEEP

While on a trip you might not always get a crib at your destination, and carrying one will make life all the more difficult. Instead call ahead to see if there are any cribs or roll out beds for children. You may even put blankets on the floor. Weave them a story about camping and they will gladly sleep without any trouble.

32. GET BABY PRODUCTS DELIVERED AT YOUR DESTINATION

If you are absolutely paranoid about not getting your favourite variety of diaper or brand of baby food, check out online stores like amazon.com for services in your destination city. You can buy things online ahead of your travel and get them delivered to your hotel upon arrival.

33. FEEDING NEEDS OF YOUR INFANTS

If you are travelling with a breastfed infant, you save the trouble of carrying bottles and bottle sanitization kits. For special food, or medications, you may need to call ahead to make sure you have a refrigerator where you are staying.

34. FEEDING NEEDS OF YOUR TODDLER

With the progression from infancy to toddler, their dietary requirements too evolve. You will have to pack some snacks for travelling time. Fresh fruits and vegetables can be purchased at your destination. Most of the cities you travel to in whichever part of the world, will have baby food products and formulas, available at the local drug-store or the supermarket.

35. PICKING CLOTHES FOR YOUR BABY

Contrary to popular belief, babies can do without many changes of clothes. At the most pack 2 outfits per day. Pack mix and match type clothes for your little one as well. Pick things which are comfortable to wear and quick to dry.

36. SELECTING SHOES FOR YOUR BABY

Like outfits, kids can make do with two pairs of comfortable shoes. If you can get some water resistant shoes it will be best. To expedite drying wet shoes, you can stuff newspaper in them then wrap them with newspaper and leave them to dry overnight.

37. KEEP ONE CHANGE OF CLOTHES HANDY

Travelling with kids can be tricky. Keep a change of clothes for the kids and mum handy in your purse or tote bag. This takes a bit of space in your hand luggage but comes extremely handy in case there are any accidents or spills.

38. LEAVE BEHIND BABY ACCESSORIES

Baby accessories like their bed, bath tub, car seat, crib etc. should be left at home. Many hotels provide a crib on request, while car seats can be borrowed from friends or rented. Babies can be given a bath in the hotel sink or even in the adult bath tub with a little bit of water. If you bring a few bath toys, they can be used in the bath, pool, and out of water. They can also be sanitized easily in the sink.

39. CARRY A SMALL LOAD OF PLASTIC BAGS

With children around there are chances of a number of soiled clothes and diapers. These plastic bags help to sort the dirt from the clean inside your big bag. These are very light weight and come in handy to other carry stuff as well at times.

PACK WITH A PURPOSE

40. PACKING FOR BUSINESS TRIPS

One neutral-colored suit should suffice. It can be paired with different shirts, ties and accessories for different occasions. One pair of black suit pants could be worn with a matching jacket for the office or with a snazzy top for dinner.

41. PACKING FOR A CRUISE

Most cruises have formal dinners, and that formal dress usually takes up a lot of space. However you might find a tuxedo to rent. For women, a short black dress with multiple accessory options will do the trick.

42. PACKING FOR A LONG TRIP OVER DIFFERENT CLIMATES

The secret packing mantra for travel over multiple climates is layering. Layering traps air around your body creating insulation against the cold. The same light t-shirt that is comfortable in a warmer climate can be the innermost layer in a colder climate.

REDUCE SOME MORE WEIGHT

43. LEAVE PRECIOUS THINGS AT HOME

Things that you would hate to lose or get damaged leave them at home. Precious jewelry, expensive gadgets or dresses, could be anything. You will not require these on your trip. Leave them at home and spare the load on your mind.

44. SEND SOUVENIRS BY MAIL

If you have spent all your money on purchasing souvenirs, carrying them back in the same bag that you brought along would be difficult. Either pack everything in another bag and check it in the airport or get everything shipped to your home. Use an international carrier for a secure transit, but this could be more expensive than the checking fees at the airport.

45. AVOID CARRYING BOOKS

Books equal to weight. There are many reading apps which you can download on your smart phone or tab. Plus there are gadgets like Kindle and Nook that are thinner and lighter alternatives to your regular book.

CHECK, GET, SET, CHECK AGAIN

46. STRATEGIZE BEFORE PACKING

Create a travel list and prepare all that you think you need to carry along. Keep everything on your bed or floor before packing and then think through once again – do I really need that? Any item that meets this question can be avoided. Remove whatever you don't really need and pack the rest.

47. TEST YOUR LUGGAGE

Once you have fully packed for the trip take a test trip with your luggage. Take your bags and go to town for window shopping for an hour. If you enjoy your hour long trip it is good to go, if not, go home and reduce the load some more. Repeat this test till you hit the right weight.

48. ADD A ROLL OF DUCT TAPE

You might wonder why, when this book has been talking about reducing stuff, we're suddenly asking you to pack something totally unusual. This is because when you have limited supplies, duct tape is immensely helpful for small repairs – a broken bag, leaking zip-lock bag, broken sunglasses, you name it and duct tape can fix it, temporarily.

49. LIST OF ESSENTIAL ITEMS

Even though the emphasis is on packing light, there are things which have to be carried for any trip. Here is our list of essentials:

- Passport/Visa or any other ID

- Any other paper work that might be required on a trip like permits, hotel reservation confirmations etc.

- Medicines – all your prescription medicines and emergency kit, especially if you are travelling with children

- Medical or vaccination records

- Money in foreign currency if travelling to a different country

- Tickets- Email or Message them to your phone

50. MAKE THE MOST OF YOUR TRIP

Wherever you are going, whatever you hope to do we encourage you to embrace it whole-heartedly. Take in the scenery, the culture and above all, enjoy your time away from home.

PACKING AND PLANNING TIPS

A Week before Leaving

- Arrange for someone to take care of pets and water plants

- Stop mail and newspaper

- Notify Credit Card companies where you are going.

- Change your thermostat settings

- Car inspected, oil is changed, and tires have the correct pressure.

- Passports and id is up to date.

- Pay bills.

- Copy important items and download travel Apps.

- Start collecting small bills for tips

Right Before Leaving

- Clean out refrigerator.

- Empty garbage cans.

- Lock windows.

- Make sure you have the right ID with you.

- Bring cash for tips.

- Remember travel documents.

- Lock door behind you.

- Remember wallet.

- Unplug items in house and pack chargers.

>TOURIST

READ OTHER
GREATER THAN A TOURIST
BOOKS

>TOURIST

> TOURIST

Visit Greater Than a Tourist for Free Travel Tips
http://GreaterThanATourist.com

Sign up for the Greater Than a Tourist Newsletter for
discount days, new books, and travel information:
http://eepurl.com/cxspyf

Follow us on Facebook for tips, images, and ideas:
https://www.facebook.com/GreaterThanATourist

Follow us on Pinterest for travel tips and ideas:
http://pinterest.com/GreaterThanATourist

Follow us on Instagram for beautiful travel images:
http://Instagram.com/GreaterThanATourist

\>TOURIST

> TOURIST

Please leave your honest review of this book on Amazon and Goodreads. Please send your feedback to GreaterThanaTourist@gmail.com as we continue to improve the series. Thank you. We appreciate your positive and constructive feedback. Thank you.

METRIC CONVERSIONS

TEMPERATURE

110° F —
100° F —   — 40° C
90° F —
80° F —   — 30° C
70° F —   — 20° C
60° F —
50° F —   — 10° C
40° F —
32° F —   — 0° C
20° F —
10° F —   — -10° C
0° F —
-10° F —   — -18° C
-20° F —   — -30° C

To convert F to C:

Subtract 32, and then multiply by 5/9 or .5555.

To Convert C to F:

Multiply by 1.8 and then add 32.

32F = 0C

LIQUID VOLUME

To Convert:...................Multiply by
U.S. Gallons to Liters................ 3.8
U.S. Liters to Gallons 26
Imperial Gallons to U.S. Gallons 1.2
Imperial Gallons to Liters....... 4.55
Liters to Imperial Gallons 22
1 Liter = .26 U.S. Gallon
1 U.S. Gallon = 3.8 Liters

DISTANCE

To convert ....Multiply by
Inches to Centimeters 2.54
Centimeters to Inches 39
Feet to Meters...................... .3
Meters to Feet 3.28
Yards to Meters 91
Meters to Yards 1.09
Miles to Kilometers 1.61
Kilometers to Miles............. .62
1 Mile = 1.6 km
1 km = .62 Miles

WEIGHT

1 Ounce = .28 Grams
1 Pound = .4555 Kilograms
1 Gram = .04 Ounce
1 Kilogram = 2.2 Pounds

TRAVEL QUESTIONS

- Do you bring presents home to family or friends after a vacation?

- Do you get motion sick?

- Do you have a favorite billboard?

- Do you know what to do if there is a flat tire?

- Do you like a sun roof open?

- Do you like to eat in the car?

- Do you like to wear sun glasses in the car?

- Do you like toppings on your ice cream?

- Do you use public bathrooms?

- Did you bring your cell phone and does it have power?

- Do you have a form of identification with you?

- Have you ever been pulled over by a cop?

- Have you ever given money to a stranger on a road trip?

- Have you ever taken a road trip with animals?

- Have you ever went on a vacation alone?

- Have you ever run out of gas?

- If you could move to any place in the world, where would it be?

- If you could travel anywhere in the world, where would you travel?

- If you could travel in any vehicle, which one would it be?

- If you had three things to wish for from a magic genie, what would they be?

- If you have a driver's license, how many times did it take you to pass the test?

- What are you the most afraid of on vacation?

- What do you want to get away from the most when you are on vacation?

- What foods smells bad to you?

- What item to you bring on ever trip with you away from home?

- What makes you sleepy?

- What song would you love to hear on the radio when you're cruising on the highway?

- What travel job would you want the least?

- What will you miss most while you are away from home?

- What is something you always wanted to try?

- What is the best road side attraction that you ever saw?

- What is the farthest distance you ever biked?

- What is the farthest distance you ever walked?

- What is the weirdest thing you needed to buy while on vacation?

- What is your favorite candy?

- What is your favorite color car?

- What is your favorite family vacation?

- What is your favorite food in the world?

- What is your favorite gas station drink or food?

- What is your favorite license plate design?

- What is your favorite restaurant in the world?

- What is your favorite smell?

- What is your favorite song?

- What is your favorite sound that nature makes?

- What is your favorite thing to bring home from a vacation?

- What is your favorite vacation with friends?

- What is your favorite way to relax?

- What is your favorite weather conditions while driving?

- Where in the world would you rather never get to travel?

- Where is the farthest place you ever traveled in a car?

- Where is the farthest place you ever went North, South, East and West?

- Where is your favorite place in the world?

- Who is your favorite singer?

- Who taught you how to drive?

- Who will you miss the most while you are away?

- Who if the first person you will call when you get to your destination?

- Who brought you on your first vacation?

- Who likes to travel the most in your life?

- Would you rather be hot or cold?

- Would you rather drive above, below, or at the speed limited?

- Would you rather drive on a highway or a back road?

- Would you rather go on a train or a boat?

- Would you rather go to the beach or the woods?

TRAVEL BUCKET LIST

NOTES